ISBN: 978-0-7390-8699-5

Visit Hal Leonard Online at
www.halleonard.com

Contact us:
Hal Leonard
7777 West Bluemound Road
Milwaukee, WI 53213
Email: info@halleonard.com

In Europe, contact:
Hal Leonard Europe Limited
42 Wigmore Street
Marylebone, London, W1U 2RN
Email: info@halleonardeurope.com

In Australia, contact:
Hal Leonard Australia Pty. Ltd.
4 Lentara Court
Cheltenham, Victoria, 3192 Australia
Email: info@halleonard.com.au

Contents

ALL MY LIFE

Moderately fast rock ♩ = 168

Words and Music by
DAVID GROHL, TAYLOR HAWKINS,
CHRIS SHIFLETT and NATE MENDEL

All My Life - 10 - 1

it come to life when I see your ghost.____

6

*Harmonic is located three tenths the distance
between 3rd and 4th frets.

Elec. Gtrs. 1, 2, 3, & 4 cont. simile

___ it comes a - round, and it's tak - en a - way.___ Leaves__ me with the feel - ing that I

feel the most,___ feel___ it come to life when I see your ghost.__ Then I'm

done, done, on to the next___ one. Done,___ done and I'm

on to the next___ one. Done,___ done and I'm on to the next___ one. Done,___

___ done and I'm on to the next___ one. Done,___ done and I'm

on to the next___ one. Done,___ done and I'm on to the next___ one. Done,___

___ done and I'm on to the next___ one. Done,___

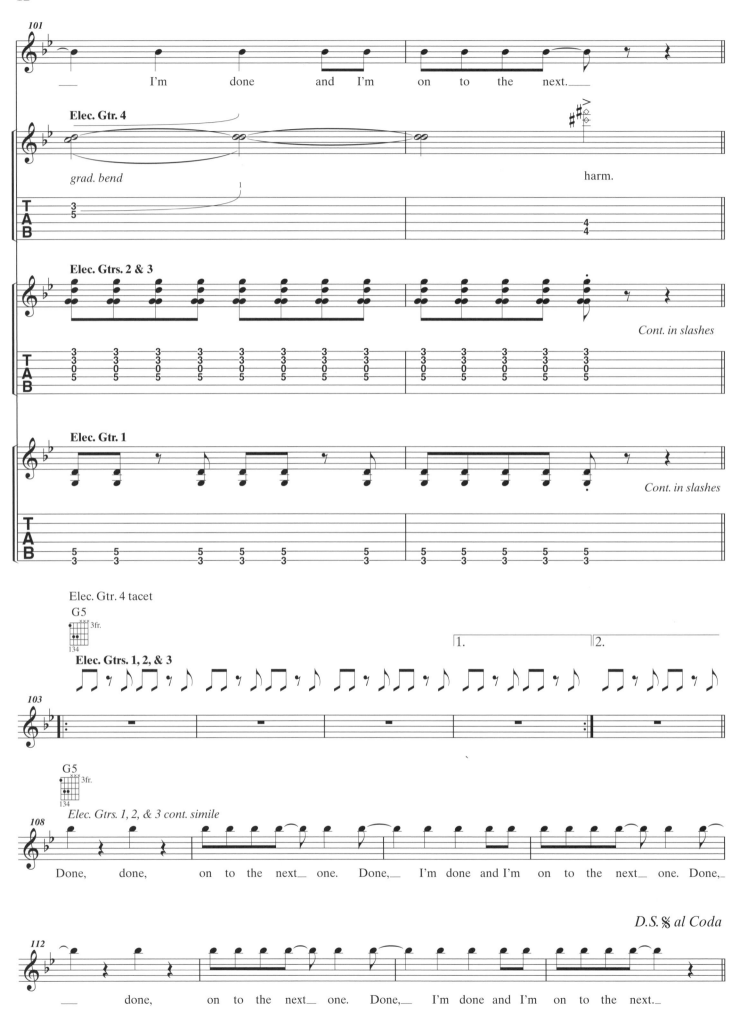

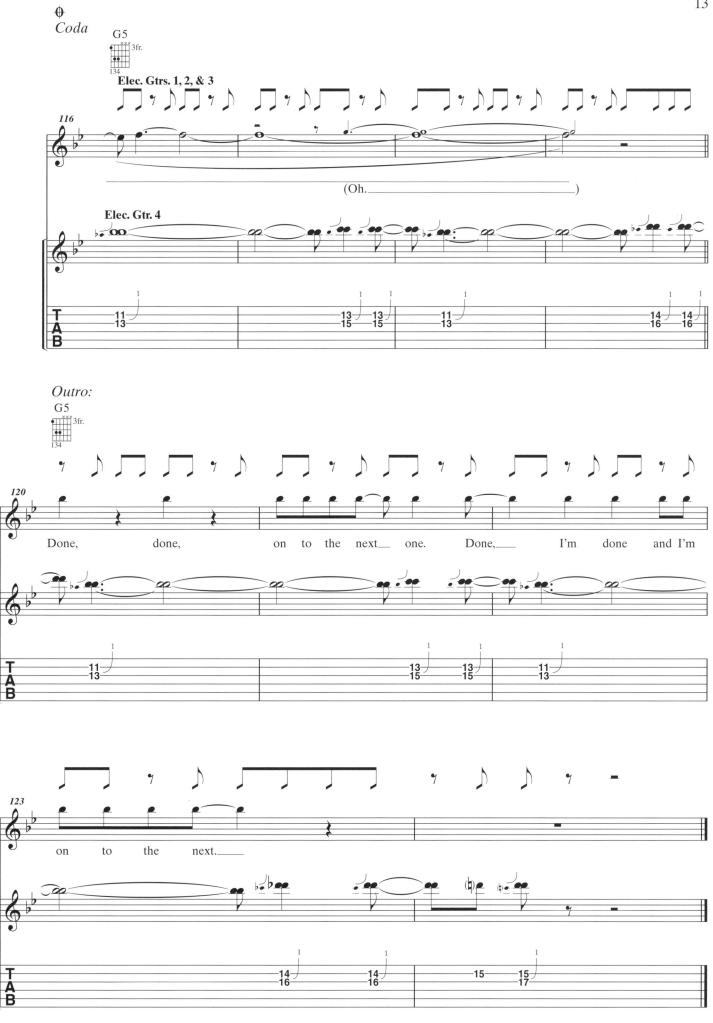

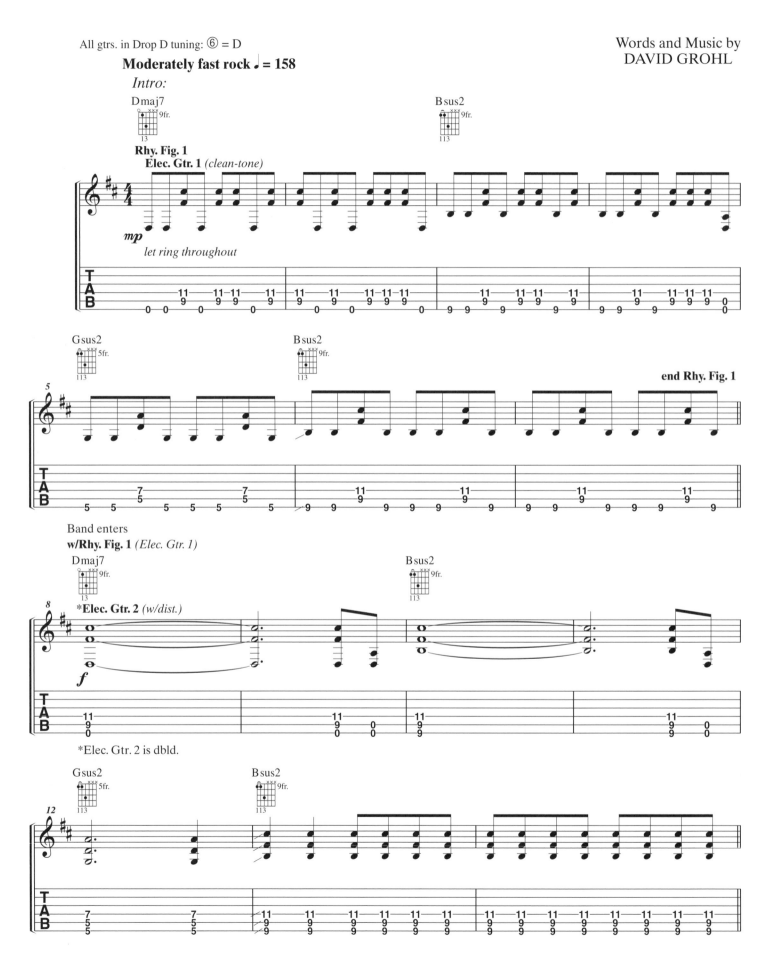

EVERLONG

*4th string is muted with left-hand index finger.

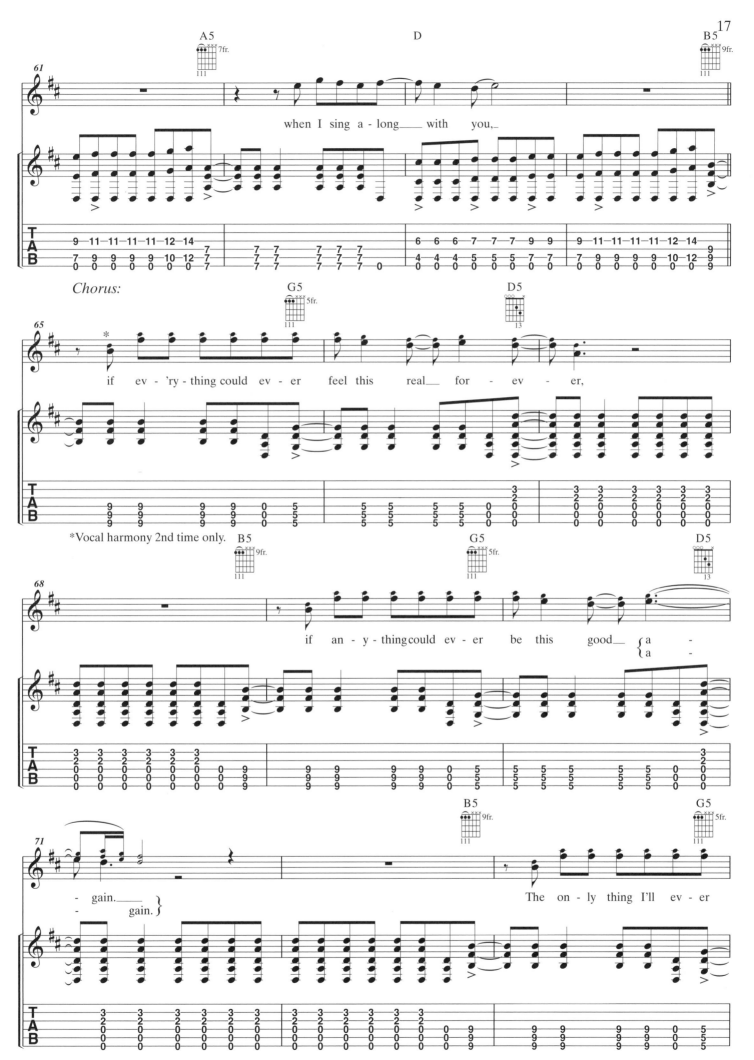

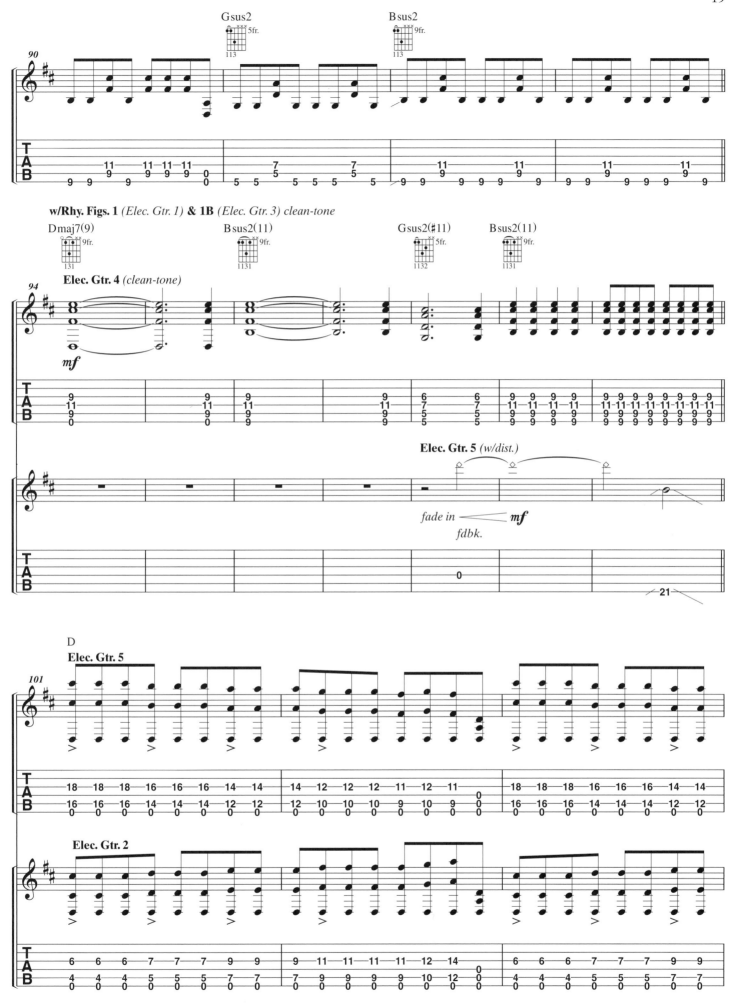

LEARN TO FLY

Words and Music by
DAVID GROHL, TAYLOR HAWKINS
and NATE MENDEL

Moderately fast rock ♩ = 136

Intro:

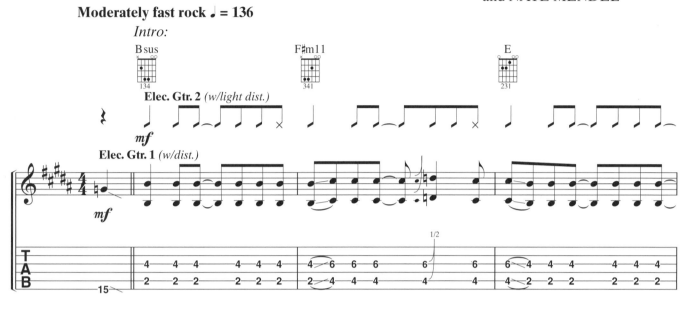

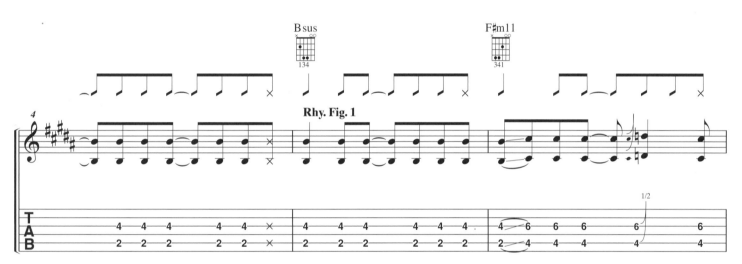

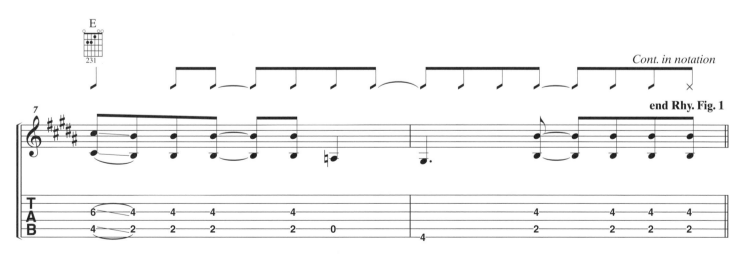

Learn to Fly - 6 - 1

MONKEY WRENCH

Words and Music by
DAVID GROHL, NATE MENDEL
and PAT SMEAR

Monkey Wrench - 9 - 1

32

34

Coda
Chorus:
w/Rhy. Figs. 1 (Elec. Gtr. 1) & 1A (Elec. Gtr. 2) both 1st 4 meas. only, 3 times each
E5 F#5 E5 C5 B5 F#5 E5
Don't wan - na be your mon - key wrench.
(Fall in, fall out.)
B5 F#5
Don't wan - na be your mon - key wrench.
E5 B5
(Fall in, fall out.)
Don't wan - na be
F#5 E5
your mon - key wrench.
(Fall in, fall
Elec. Gtr. 2 tacet
B5 F#5 E5 F#5 E5 F#5
out.)
Don't wan - na be your mon - key wrench.
Elec. Gtr. 1
E5 D5 F#5 E5 D5 F#5 E5 D5 F#5 E5 C5 B5

MY HERO

Words and Music by
DAVID GROHL, NATE MENDEL
and PAT SMEAR

38

Verse 3:

Elec. Gtr. 2 resume intro fig. simile

Ku - dos,__ my__ he - ro;__ leav-in' all__ the best._____

Elec. Gtr. 1

You know__ my__ he - ro,_____ the one that's on._____

THE PRETENDER

Words and Music by
DAVID GROHL, TAYLOR HAWKINS,
CHRIS SHIFLETT and NATE MENDEL

The Pretender - 10 - 1

end half-time feel

*Chord is implied.

Verse 1:

w/Rhy. Fig. 2 (Elec. Gtr. 1) 8 times

Elec. Gtr. 2 (w/light dist.)

Send in___ your skel - e - tons.___ Sing as___ their bones___ come march - ing in___

a - gain.___

Rhy. Fig. 3

The need___ you bur - ied deep,___ the se - crets that___ you keep are

The Pretender - 10 - 3

44

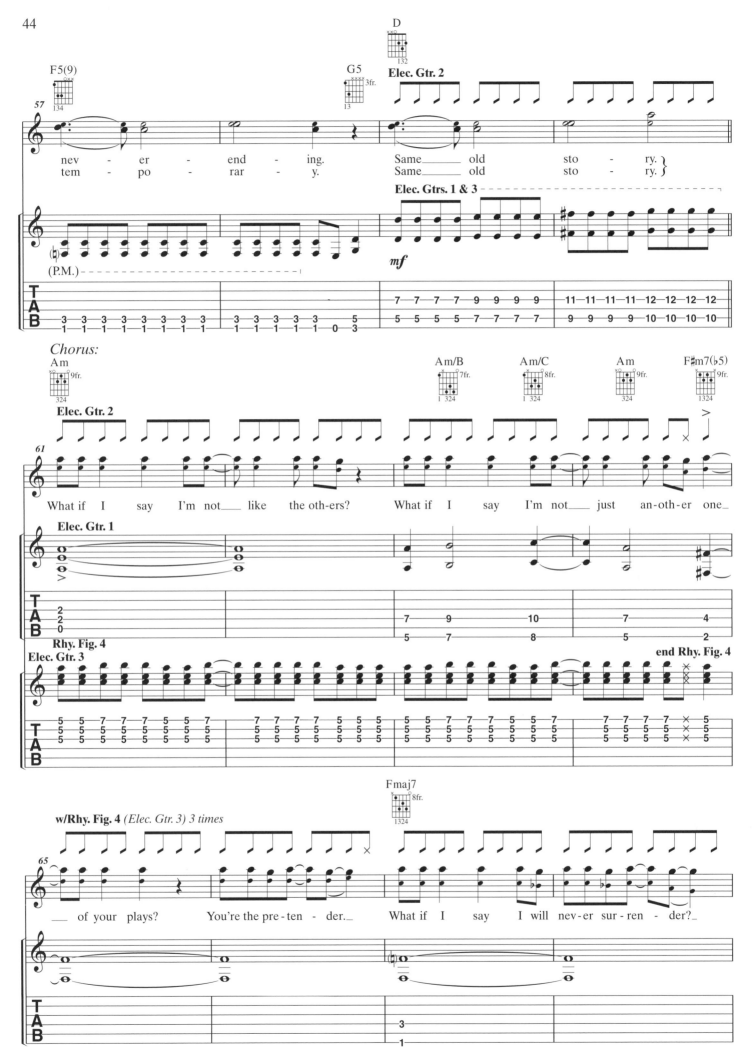

The Pretender - 10 - 4

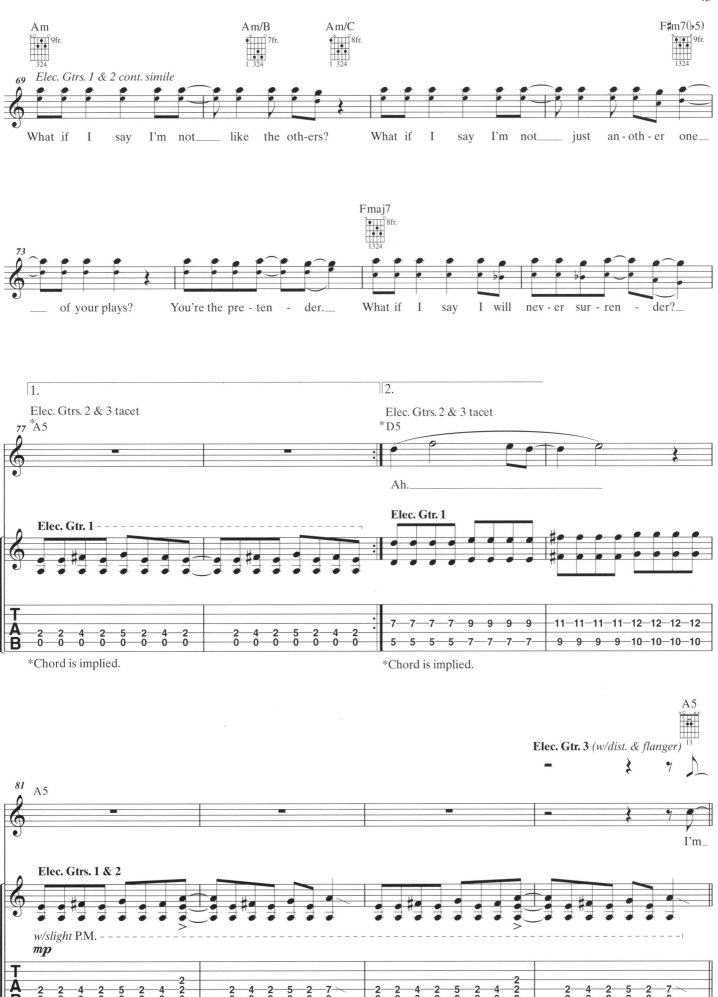

46

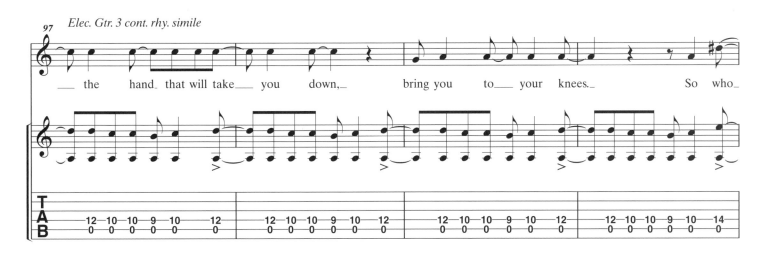

the hand that will take_ you down,_ bring you to_ your knees._ So who_

_ are you?_ Yeah, who_ are you?_ Yeah, who_

_ are you?_ Yeah, who_ are you?_

Resume half-time feel
Band tacet 8 meas.
w/Rhy. Fig. 1A _(Elec. Gtr. 1) see meas. 17–24_

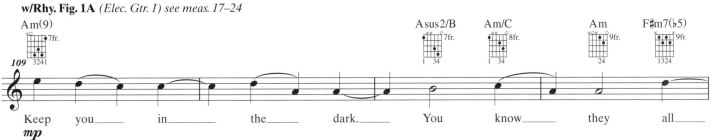

Keep you_ in_ the_ dark._ You know_ they all_

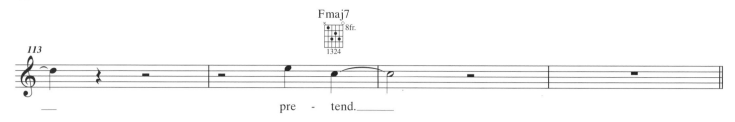

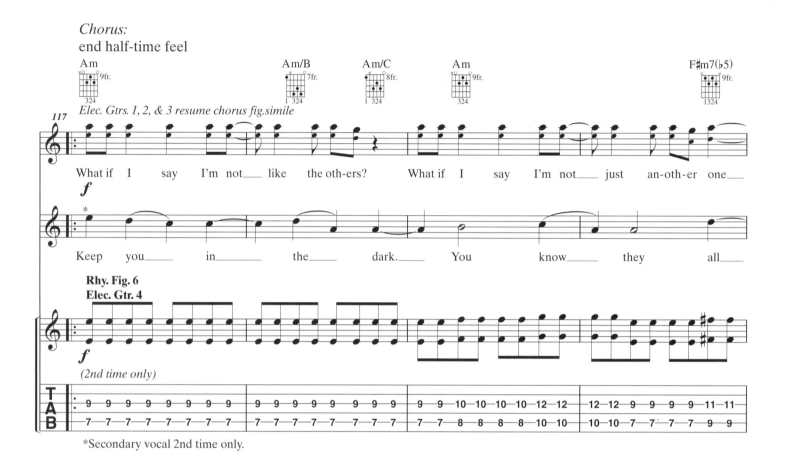

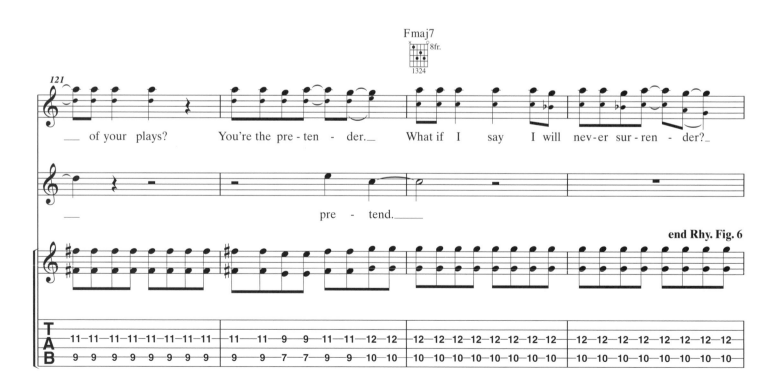

50

Outro:

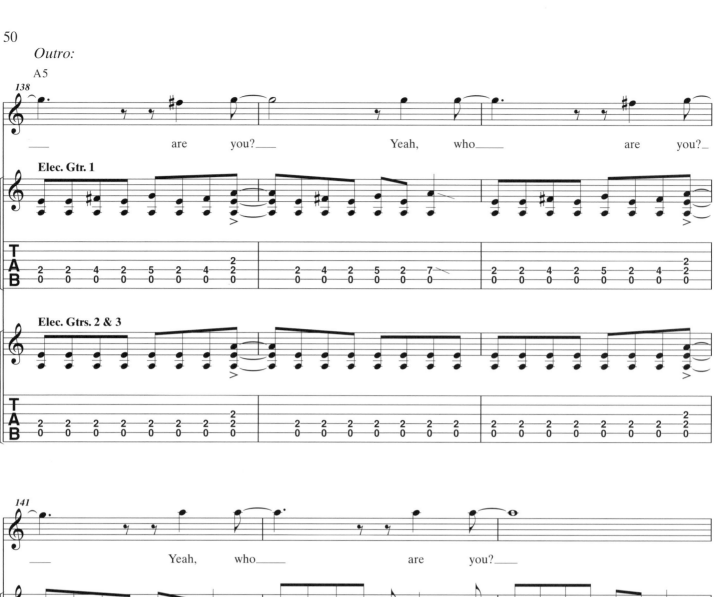

TIMES LIKE THESE

Words and Music by
DAVID GROHL, TAYLOR HAWKINS,
CHRIS SHIFLETT and NATE MENDEL

*Chord names are implied.

Times Like These - 9 - 1

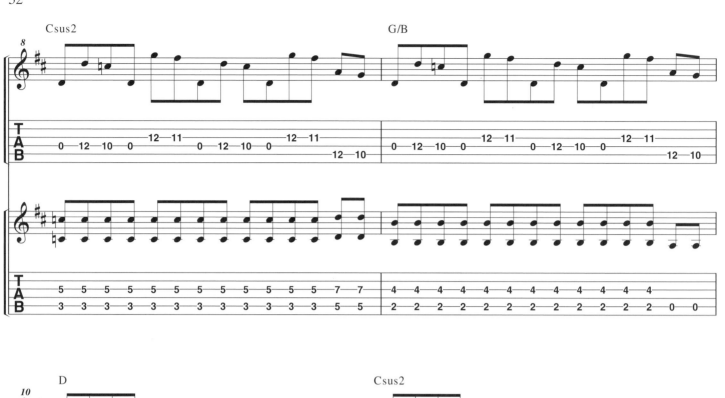

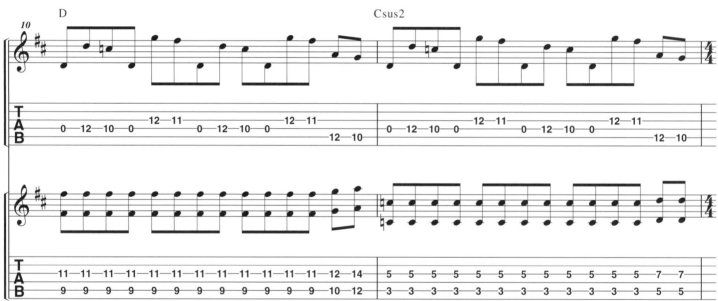

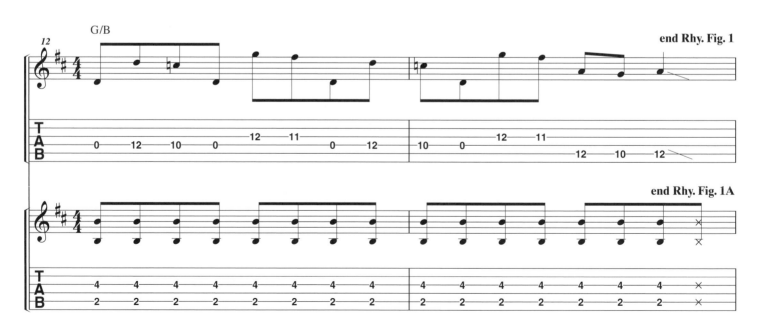

Uh.___
Uh.___

It's   times_

Chorus:

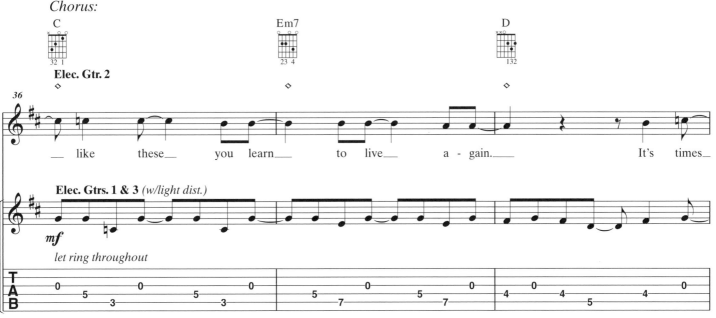

C   Em7   D

Elec. Gtr. 2

___ like these___ you learn___ to live___ a - gain.___   It's   times_

Elec. Gtrs. 1 & 3 *(w/light dist.)*

mf

let ring throughout

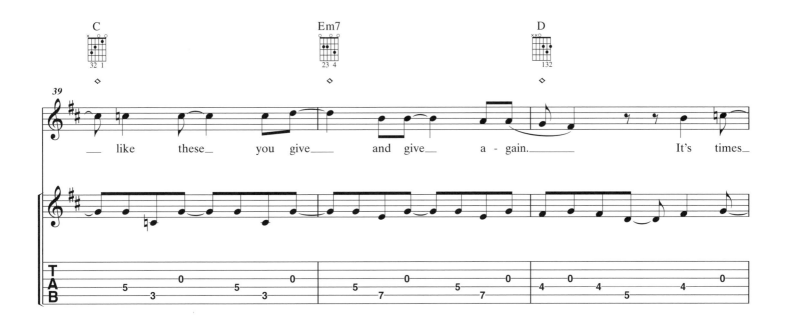

C   Em7   D

___ like these___ you give___ and give___ a - gain.___   It's   times_

58

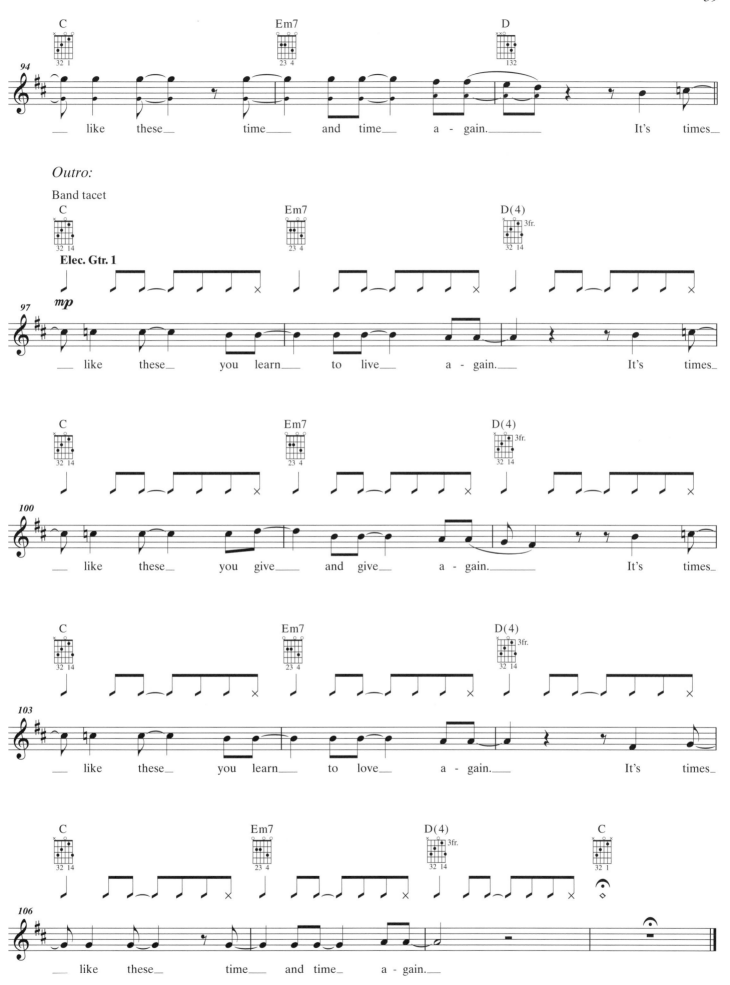

WALK

Moderately ♩ = 132

Intro:

Words and Music by
DAVID GROHL, TAYLOR HAWKINS,
CHRIS SHIFLETT, NATE MENDEL
and PAT SMEAR

Verse 1:

Walk - 11 - 1

Verse 2:

Dm6/A
Asus2
whom it may con - cern.
I think I lost my way.
end Rhy. Fig. 2
E
Esus
Bm7
7fr.
Elec. Gtr. 1
Get-ting good at start - ing o -
Dm6
Dm7
5fr.
- ver ev - 'ry time that I re - turn.

Cont. in notation

Bm7

I be-lieve___ I've wait-ed long e-nough. Where do I___

*Vocal harmony of D.S. only.

A
Elec. Gtrs. 1 & 3

Dm
Elec. Gtr. 2

___ be-gin?___ I'm learn-ing to talk___ a-gain.

Elec. Gtrs. 1 & 3

Cont. in slashes

E   Bm7

{ I be-lieve___ I've wait-ed long
{ Can't you see___ I've wait-ed long

Walk - 11 - 6

70

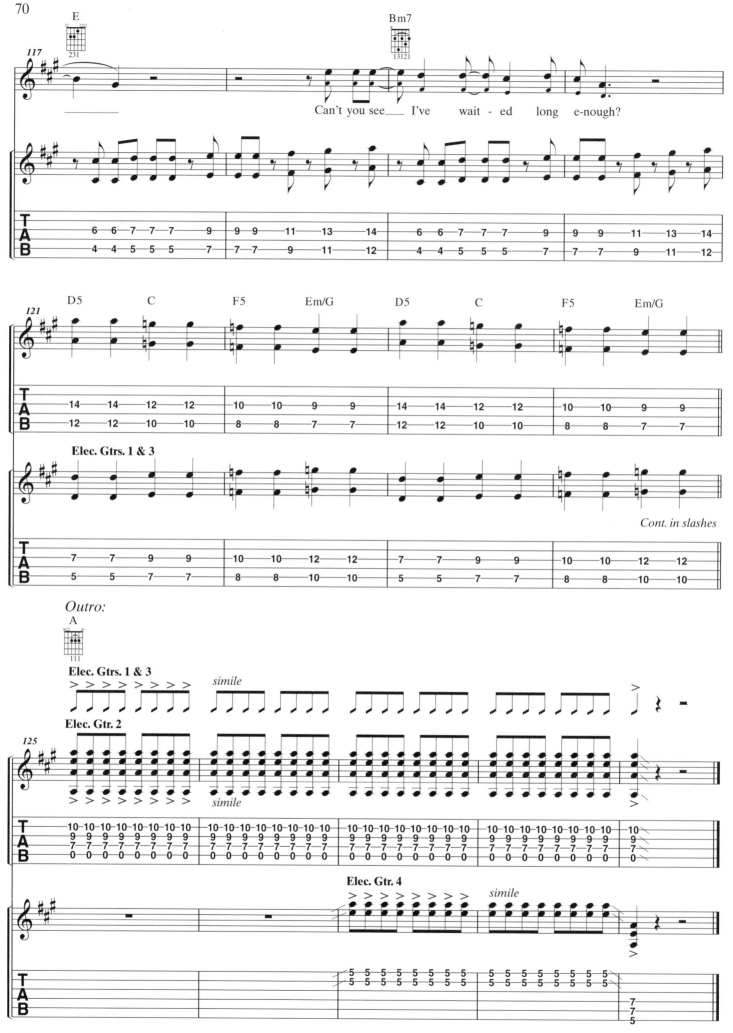

Can't you see___ I've wait-ed long e-nough?

Outro:

Walk - 11 - 11

TABLATURE EXPLANATION

TAB illustrates the six strings of the guitar.
Notes and chords are indicated by the placement of fret numbers on each string.

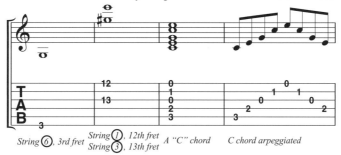

String ⑥, 3rd fret   String ①, 12th fret   A "C" chord   C chord arpeggiated
String ③, 13th fret

BENDING NOTES

Half Step:
Play the note and bend
string one half step
(one fret).

Whole Step:
Play the note and bend
string one whole step
(two frets).

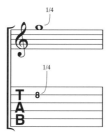

**Slight Bend/
Quarter-Tone Bend:**
Play the note and bend
string sharp.

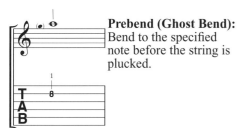

Prebend (Ghost Bend):
Bend to the specified
note before the string is
plucked.

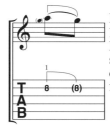

**Prebend and
Release:**
Play the already-bent
string, then immediately
drop it down to the
fretted note.

Unison Bends:
Play both notes and
immediately bend the
lower note to the same
pitch as the higher note.

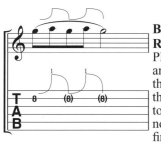

**Bend and
Release:**
Play the note
and bend to
the next pitch,
then release
to the original
note. Only the
first note is
attacked.

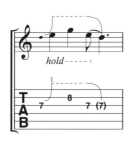

**Bends Involving
More Than One
String:**
Play the note and
bend the string
while playing an
additional note
on another string.
Upon release, re-
lieve the pressure from the additional note
allowing the original note to sound alone.

**Bends Involving
Stationary Notes:**
Play both notes and
immediately bend the
lower note up to pitch.
Return as indicated.

ARTICULATIONS

Hammer On:
Play the lower note, then "hammer" your finger to the higher note. Only the first note is plucked.

Pull Off:
Play the higher note with your first finger already in position on the lower note. Pull your finger off the first note with a strong downward motion that plucks the string—sounding the lower note.

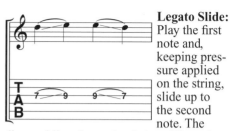

Legato Slide:
Play the first note and, keeping pressure applied on the string, slide up to the second note. The diagonal line shows that it is a slide and not a hammer-on or a pull-off.

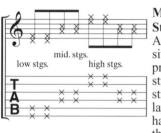

Muted Strings:
A percussive sound is produced by striking the strings while laying the fret hand across them.

Palm Mute:
The notes are muted (muffled) by placing the palm of the pick hand lightly on the strings, just in front of the bridge.

HARMONICS

Natural Harmonic:
A finger of the fret hand lightly touches the string at the note indicated in the TAB and is plucked by the pick producing a bell-like sound called a harmonic.

RHYTHM SLASHES

Strum Marks/ Rhythm Slashes:
Strum with the indicated rhythm pattern. Strum marks can be located above the staff or within the staff.

Single Notes with Rhythm Slashes:
Sometimes single notes are incorporated into a strum pattern. The circled number below is the string and the fret number is above.

Artificial Harmonic:
Fret the note at the first TAB number, lightly touch the string at the fret indicated in parens (usually 12 frets higher than the fretted note), then pluck the string with an available finger or your pick.

TREMOLO BAR

Specified Interval:
The pitch of a note or chord is lowered to the specified interval and then return as indicated. The action of the tremolo bar is graphically represented by the peaks and valleys of the diagram.

Unspecified Interval:
The pitch of a note or chord is lowered, usually very dramatically, until the pitch of the string becomes indeterminate.

PICK DIRECTION

Downstrokes and Upstrokes:
The downstroke is indicated with this symbol (⊓) and the upstroke is indicated with this (V).